THE USE OF SYMBOLISM
IN CHRISTIAN EDUCATION

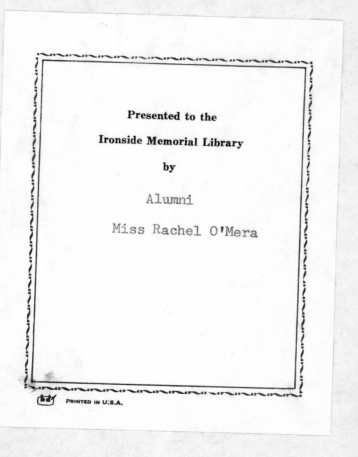

BOOKS BY DOROTHY B. FRITZ
Published by The Westminster Press

The Spiritual Growth of Children
Activity Programs for Junior Groups

THE USE OF SYMBOLISM IN CHRISTIAN EDUCATION

By

Dorothy B. Fritz

THE WESTMINSTER PRESS
Philadelphia

PRINTED IN THE UNITED STATES OF AMERICA

26721

PREFACE

The interest of which this book is a result began with considerable involvement with drama, especially church-centered drama. The whole field of expression of Christian concepts in various art forms was further opened up in the classes of Harry Mason, particularly those in worship and color symbolism. In the extensive library at Auburn—both when I attended the seminary in upper New York State and later when it was moved to Union Seminary in New York City—I read every book I could find on the subject—far too many to acknowledge, and many of them now out of print. Impetus was given to this by the rich resources in the libraries at Princeton Theological Seminary and Princeton University while doing part-time teaching in the seminary.

It was at Princeton, too, that I met the late Dr. Walter Lowrie, whose interest and advice during several conversations brought the whole matter into focus. He shared my feeling that to find the material relevant to our Reformed faith meant doing an amount of reading that told the reader more than he wanted to know—historically, technically, and eccleasiastically! Mr. Henry Lee Willet, of the Willet Stained Glass Studios in Philadelphia, was also most helpful.

The books listed in the Bibliography at the end of this book will be helpful to those who wish to carry their study much farther than this small handbook attempts to do. They are, in the main, a part of the present "mood," and much more selective than those read over the years of preparation for this writing. The chart at the end of Chapter IV appeared originally in the magazine *Discovery* (July-September, 1951).

DOROTHY B. FRITZ

CONTENTS

INTRODUCTION

Throughout the Protestant Church there is an increasing interest in symbolism. During the early days of Protestantism and the breaking away of state churches from the domination of the Roman Church, two courses were followed. In certain church groups, much of the liturgy and symbolism in church art, architecture, and vestments continued to be used. The break was largely governmental. In varying degrees this was true of the Lutheran churches, the Anglican, the Protestant Episcopal, and the Methodist churches.

In other religious groups, largely those in the Reformed tradition, sharp differences in theology and procedures led to a sterner simplicity in church buildings and in the forms of worship held in them. Communication of the faith centered in words—the words of Scripture and sermon, of prayer and hymn. Even the cross was seldom used—the sacraments of Baptism and the Lord's Supper were almost the only remaining symbols.

The tradition of drastic simplicity has persisted among such groups as the Quakers and the Mennonites; but what happened in other churches can hardly be dignified by the word "symbolism" or compared to any other medieval art form. It was, in most cases, piously oriented decoration, ugly and meaningless. "Art glass" replaced clear windows, but with none of the rich response to changing light that made stained glass so glorious. The use of color and line had no meaning. The intent to make the faith visible to an inquiring mind, as a book that can be read, was lost.

So, in the early days of Christian education, little was done to acquaint the congregation, or the children and young people being nurtured in the faith, with any forms of Christian symbolism. Teaching, too, became almost wholly a matter of words, with no effective use made of the possibilities in communication through our rich heritage of Christian liturgy and art forms.

But now there is a new appreciation throughout the Reformed churches of what they have put aside for so many years. As the people in the churches and the professional architects and builders they employed searched for ways to create buildings, designed with dignity, beauty, and meaning, worthy of housing the worship of God, a return to the past was inevitable. Gothic churches and modified forms of Gothic appeared everywhere.

Only recently, both here and abroad, have new ways of expressing the old, old concepts begun to emerge. Oddly enough this has happened most frequently in the churches that stayed closest to traditional ecclesiastical forms down through the years—Lutheran, Roman Catholic, Anglican. But as the old or new art forms are used with real meaning, the necessity for a constant reinterpretation of that meaning is also clear.

So we have excellent new books for the interpretation of Christian symbols, architecture, and art forms (see the Bibliography at the end of the book). We have teaching concerning them in current curriculum materials and in all types of activities and projects. We have excursions for such teaching not only through our own particular church, but to churches of other traditions, including Jewish synagogues and homes in which so much of our common Biblical background comes to life in visible forms and observances.

But always we need to be reminded that symbolism is a valid part of Christian experience only when our symbols express our deepest meanings, and when such meanings are understood by those who live with them.

I

THE MEANING
OF SYMBOLISM

If you were to look in the public library of a large city, in the reference sections marked "Art" or "Architecture," you would find many books on symbolism. Most of them are old; the type is small and difficult to read; the illustrations are from uninteresting steel engravings. You would find these books, in the main, very dull reading—technical, and crowded with ecclesiastical detail. It is as if you were to enter a great cathedral, and were forced to go over it inch by inch, to understand each chisel mark, each carved leaf, each tiny piece of stained glass. You would no doubt have to search, in either book or cathedral, for days and weeks and months to find one or two symbols that have meaning to you as a person in the Reformed tradition—a Protestant.

But there is a clear-cut line of development of symbolism in Protestant Christianity; knowledge of it can enrich our heritage immeasurably, making the walls of even the simplest church building speak to us of our faith. That is what the builder intends to do for the worshiper; to become acquainted with the meaning of symbols is a way of learning a language in wood and stone, in glass and metal, in tapestries, in lights and color.

What Is a Symbol?

The word "symbol" comes from a Greek root meaning "to throw with." It means putting together an abstract idea and a visible object, so that the object stands for, or represents, the idea or concept. From the earliest days of God's chosen people there has been

11

a clear-cut edict against the kind of direct representation that is idolatry. Pagan religions have long made such direct representation of their gods. A picture or statue of *our* God is unthinkable, and was, in fact, expressly forbidden (Ex. 20:4). But the triple circle as a *symbol* of God is merely an attempt to express the inexpressible, in so far as we are able. Just so the early Hebrews would not speak the "name" of God, for fear of irreverent familiarity, but used many terms that they understood to *mean* God (Ex. 3:14).

The Use of Symbols Is Universal

Symbolism is clearly a language used in all ages, by all peoples. In some respects it is universal. For instance, all around the world there is a common acceptance of "up" to express desirable, and "down" to express undesirable, happenings.

We are surrounded by symbols. Indeed, they are so generally used that even very young children recognize the colors that mean "stop" or "go," the warning and direction symbols that line our highways, the flags and seals of state and nation, the red, white, and blue of our letter boxes, the green cross that gives a doctor special parking privileges, and the red cross that symbolizes help in disaster areas.

The use of symbolism is sanctioned by both Biblical and ecclesiastical authority. The Bible is full of symbolism, much of it difficult for us but clear to the Hebrews, who thought and spoke in elaborate symbols. Psalm 23 is entirely symbolism; in Ps. 51 we find both the symbols and the idea symbolized as we contrast verses seven and ten: "Purge me with hyssop, and I shall be clean; wash me, and I shall be whiter than snow" (v. 7); "Create in me a clean heart, O God, and put a new and right spirit within me" (v. 10). God himself used symbols and directed their use—the flaming sword (Gen. 3:24), the mark of Cain (Gen. 4:15), the rainbow (Gen. 9:13), the blood of the Passover (Ex. 12:7, 13), the Ark of the Covenant (Ex. 25:8, 16). Always there has been and will be this attempt to put concepts beyond our powers of literal or realistic expression in terms that help us come closer to an understanding of them.

Christian symbolism developed as men sought a form of understandable expression for great religious concepts and experiences. Symbols were used long before there were Christian church build-

ings, and they were never intended for decoration—there was
nothing to decorate! The first real Christian symbols were *acts*—
baptism and the Lord's Supper. In these acts, quite simply and natu-
rally, objects were used—water, bread, wine, a chalice or cup. And
so the foundations for Christian symbolism were laid.

The Purpose and Meaning of Christian Symbols

The purpose of the first Christian symbols expressed in art forms
was identification or comfort. The early Christians found themselves
increasingly persecuted, first by their fellow Jews and later by the
Roman state. They needed a secret way of recognizing other
Christians, of identifying the places where a hunted people could
meet in comparative safety to find strength in fellowship with one
another and with their Master. It was natural that such "marks"
would be taken from the name of Jesus and from his words and
deeds, as we shall see later.

Therefore, for our present purpose, a symbol is that which con-
tains for us a Christian meaning beyond what we actually hear or
see, because of some previous knowledge or experience. The symbol
can be an object, a picture, a design, an act, a person, or even a
story. Most of the parables of Jesus were symbols in story form. The
lost sheep of Luke 15:3–7 will always mean to us the seeking, forgiving love of God. But to the uninstructed the parable describes
but a natural incident—familiar or unfamiliar, as the case may be.
And therein lies the basic peril of symbolism: that too often we
forget to explain, to constantly reinterpret our symbols, whether they
(1) give directions as road signs, red and green lights, house numbers; (2) recall personal experiences as a wedding ring, a flower, a
song, the fragrance of fresh-baked bread; or (3) express an idea or
ideal as the fourfold life symbol, the Gothic arch, a steeple, the
symbolic use of color.

None of these are of any intrinsic value except as experience, asso-
ciation, or teaching gives them meaning. To illustrate, in my living
room is a chair—one of a type found in many homes that have in-
herited early American furniture. To me, it is not merely a chair. It
is a symbol of many happy hours spent reading and talking with my
grandfather, whom I dearly loved. But to my child it would be just

a chair, unless I were able to reproduce for that child something of my experience with it.

After the years of intense persecution were over, and the Christian church was firmly established, the basic purpose of Christian symbolism became educational. Like music in the church, it was not an end in itself but a means to an end—to express religious truth, to teach sound doctrine, to lead to a response from the mind and heart to God. Books were scarce and expensive; few people could read. Therefore churches increasingly became richly illustrated and colored textbooks of Bible teaching, and of the history and doctrines of the church. But in the great cathedrals of the Middle Ages the use of symbols began to go far from the original purpose of making Biblical truth clear.

Roman Symbolism Discarded

Partly because of this—although motives were badly mixed—there came periods during which the churches were stripped of all "popish" symbols, along with stone carvings, statues, tapestries, altars. Much that was beautiful and meaningful was burned, dumped into marshes, made into tombstones, piled up to make cowsheds or sheepfolds. In surroundings of stern simplicity decreed in England, successively, by Henry VIII, Edward VI, Elizabeth, and Cromwell, the teaching of the church was done in three-hour sermons and in widespread reading of the Bible, as translation, printing, and education made this possible. In greater or lesser degree the same tendency spread over Europe, among the Reformers.

And so the church came to America, stripped of its ancient symbols as well as of those of less sound meaning which through the years had gathered like barnacles on a ship. A church just escaped from Roman Catholic persecution had little use for symbols associated with its persecutors; but the symbols of the early church and of the Biblical truth on which it was based were thrown aside with the rest—music, ritual, everything except words, the words of the preacher and of Scripture.

Today the pendulum, having touched two extremes, seems to be coming into balance. Protestant churches are slowly developing a new use of Christian symbols in which the elaborate and sentimental

LEGE

Office

ress Report

ions

cess completed! Aren't you getting
le to act on your application
en received. Please see that the
s possible.

ipt. Please request that
on as possible.

pt. Please request that
on as possible.

or other Christian worker

_____

246 - M45t

Ref. 230. G / Wilson's Dictionary
W 64qw / of Bible Types
(dark blue)
(can't take out
of library)

Ref 368:363

246 M65u

246 Ht65s

246 g g8Tttu #

Numbers

is still scorned, but which makes a place once more for a simple and dignified, but rich and colorful, symbolism, soundly based on the gospel of Jesus Christ as proclaimed through the Reformed faith. It is to the historical development and meaning of such symbols and their proper use today that we here address ourselves.

"Christian art is the expression of Christianity. We must recall it is not beauty we are striving for in art, but an honest expression of our thoughts, emotions, imaginations, and ideals.

"A vigorous Christianity will demand to be vigorously expressed, just as a sentimental Christianity will be satisfied to be expressed sentimentally. We can safely leave beauty to shift for itself. If our souls are beautiful, our purposes intelligent, and our art honestly expressed, then beauty will surely appear.

"Let us then, seek not to express our Christianity beautifully, but rather to express it honestly and skillfully in whatever media we use." *(The Arts of the Church,* Richard H. Ritter, p. 6.)

II

THE DEVELOPMENT
OF CHRISTIAN SYMBOLS

Symbols of Identification

Among the earliest symbols (as we have noted) were those of identification; marks by which, without danger, Christians might recognize their brothers in the faith.

The most familiar of these is ichthus—the fish. In the Greek the first letters of the phrase "Jesus Christ, Son of God, Savior" formed the word for "fish." The fish was often in the form of a dolphin.

IXΘYC

The fish symbol was used in many ways; for instance, to mark a house in which the Lord's Supper was to be secretly celebrated. Sometimes, when used for this purpose, there was in the mouth of the fish a crude chalice, or a small loaf of bread.

To the fish were gradually added objects that Jesus had identified with himself in his teaching, such as the lamb, the cup, bread, door, light, together with the Greek and Roman letters that identified him.

"The next day he saw Jesus coming toward him, and said, 'Behold, the Lamb of God, who takes away the sin of the world!' " (John 1:29.)

Jesus said to him, "Whoever drinks of the water that I shall give him will never thirst; the water that I shall give him will become in him a spring of water welling up to eternal life." (John 4:14.)

"Jesus said to them, 'I am the bread of life; he who comes to me shall not hunger, and he who believes in me shall never thirst.' " (John 6:35.)

"So Jesus again said to them,
. . . 'I am the door; if any one
enters by me, he will be saved.' "
(John 10:7–9.)

"Again Jesus spoke to them,
saying, 'I am the light of the
world; he who follows me will not
walk in darkness, but will have the
light of life.' " (John 8:12.)

Chi Rho is more a monogram
than a true symbol. It is made of
the first two letters of the Greek
word for "Christ."

IHS is a Roman form of monogram, representing the words "Iesus Hominum Salvator"— Jesus, Savior of Men; or the first three letters of the Greek word "Jesus" (Iota Eta Sigma).

Another symbol for Jesus Christ was the familiar anchor— a disguised form of the cross.

"We have this as a sure and steadfast anchor of the soul, a hope that enters into the inner shrine behind the curtain, where Jesus has gone as a forerunner on our behalf, having become a high priest for ever after the order of Melchizedek." (Heb. 6:19–20.)

An interesting symbol of the kind with which we are not so familiar was the figure of the pelican, that strange bird which gives of its own blood for its young.

Symbols of Comfort

The earliest use of Christian symbols centered not around forms of identification only, but around the need of the early Christians to find strength and courage to face ridicule and persecution. It was the Good Shepherd that meant most to these hunted people, scattered in all directions, huddled in darkened rooms or in the catacombs.

The figure of a shepherd bearing a lamb in his arms was used at a very early date. Symbols of God's love, his protecting care, the fellowship of suffering with the "Lamb of God" all brought comfort to distressed people.

The use of the cross as a symbol was a later development. Perhaps it was considered too sacred to use as a symbol, or perhaps its absence was a part of an early avoidance of symbols of suffering. Too many Christians were experiencing the scourge and the cross, and other forms of torture and death, to need reminders of them.

Although the symbols of Christ's Passion were not widely used until the fourth or fifth century, the resurrection symbols appeared early and often. The promise of eternal life with God, of a resurrection in and with Christ was a vital doctrine to those who daily faced death in many horrible forms.

Interestingly, many of the Bible stories, illustrated by crude pictures such as those found in the catacombs, were to these early Christians symbols of the resurrection. The creation of Adam and Eve; the emergence of Noah from the ark, of Moses from the bulrushes, of Daniel from the lion's den, of Shadrach, Meshach and Abednego from the fiery furnace, of Jonah from the "great fish," and of Lazarus from the graveclothes—these and more were used by the early Christians to symbolize the victory that was theirs over any type of suffering or death.

"And the Lord spoke to the fish, and it vomited out Jonah upon the dry land." (Jonah 2:10.)

Another very early figure is the *orans*—a figure, usually a woman, with hands outstretched in prayer. The early Christians had learned from Jesus and his disciples and from experience their own need of prayer and the power of prayer.

The Cross as a Symbol

At a later period Clement of Alexandria told the Christians to wear rings engraved with identification symbols such as the cross. (They were to wear these rings on the little finger of the *left* hand so the rings would not hinder them in their work!) And Tertullian was to say of the cross, "At every action we begin, in coming in and in going out, when we clothe ourselves or put on our shoes, when we bathe, when we seat ourselves at table, at lamplighting, on going to bed, we trace on the forehead the sign of the cross."

Gradually the cross as a symbol was recognized to be in many of the common things of life—in nature, in the form of the human body, in a variety of objects. While direct representation of the cross was not at all common until the fourth century, by the tenth century it had surpassed all other symbols. Since then, in the various streams of the Christian tradition, more than four hundred representations of the cross have developed. Those best known to us are:

The Latin Cross — which is nearest the actual form of the cross on which Christ died. In the Protestant tradition it is empty because a living rather than a dead Christ is worshiped.

The Graded Cross—the Latin cross on three steps, which represent in descending order faith, hope, and love. This is the form usually found on a Communion table.

The Cross and Crown—representing victory over death and the eternal sovereignty of Christ, as well as redemption for the faithful.

The Celtic Cross—which combined the Latin cross with the circle, the symbol of eternity. This type of cross was first made in Ireland, in about the fifth century, by men converted by St. Patrick. They carved great blocks of stone into the bold design of cross and circle. Fine examples are found on the island of Iona.

The symbol combining the Greek alpha and omega, "the beginning and the end," is used for Christ, and as a symbol of the eternal God.

Along with the increasing use of the cross came other symbols of Christ's Passion, such as the scourge, nails, crown of thorns, spear, sponge.

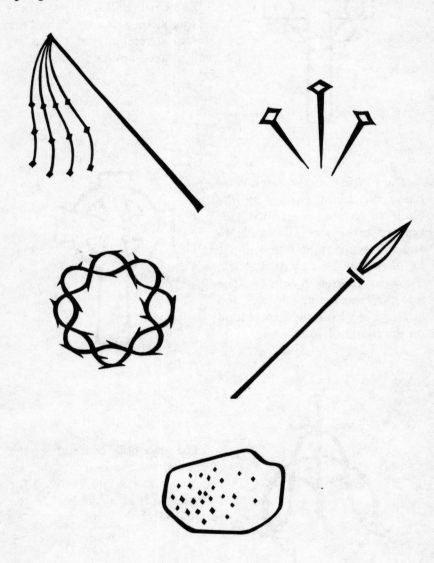

Symbols of the Trinity

As the doctrines of the church took form, it was clear that the only way Christians could express what is inexpressible—the nature of God—was in the Trinity.

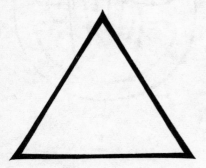

The equilateral triangle often appeared in the catacombs as a symbol of this triune God—Father, Son, and Holy Spirit, three in one, equal, eternal.

Later the trefoil and the fleur-de-lis were used. If a nimbus (halo) was part of a symbol of any one of the Godhead, there were three rays in it—a reminder of the other members of it.

There were, of course, symbols of God the Father. The most common form was the hand of God, reaching downward and open to bless mankind. Often this hand was enclosed in the circle of eternity.

The third member of the Godhead, the Holy Spirit, has been most often represented by the descending dove mentioned in the Baptism of Jesus (Matt. 3:16–17).

The tongues of flame at Pentecost (Acts 2:3).

Symbols of the Church

Two other symbols are important to Protestant Christians. One
is the ship, a symbol of Christ's
church. The sail seems to be
mounted on a cross; sometimes
above it is the banner of victory
—victory over life and death.

The other is the vine, the symbol Christ himself gave us to show
the relationship between the be-
liever, himself, and God the
Father, and the utter dependence
of man upon that relationship to
live and "bear fruit."

The Evangelists

A somewhat more complex series of symbols are those commonly
used to indicate the four Evangelists, or Gospel writers. They are
as follows:

Matthew — the winged man. His Gospel begins with the human genealogy of Jesus (Matt. 1:1).

Mark—the winged lion. Mark's Gospel speaks of Christ's kingly character, represented by the lion, the king of beasts. His book begins with ringing words from Isaiah (Mark 1:3).

Luke—the winged ox. Luke's Gospel emphasizes the sacrificial nature of Christ's death (Luke 23:35; Gal. 1:4), represented by an animal offered in the ritual of sacrifice (Heb. 13:11).

John—the eagle. It soars beyond other birds, thus symbolizing Christ's divine nature (John 14:8 –11), which John's Gospel expresses in the most exalted terms.

III

SPECIAL ASPECTS
OF SYMBOLISM

Symbolism in the Church Building

Through the years there grew up a very complicated system of symbols, most of which can be omitted here. The ones so far described are a vital part of Protestant Christianity. Also, there came to be symbols of line and color accepted by those who built churches, but seldom understood by the lay worshiper. They are meaningful only as they are rightly used and constantly reinterpreted. It is well to know some of the language of church architecture so that every church can to some extent be a reminder of God's Word to the worshiper.

Many early churches were built in the form of a cross, with the chancel as its head and the transepts as arms. It is of interest that the word "nave" (the main part of the building) is derived from the Latin word meaning "ship" (*navis*).

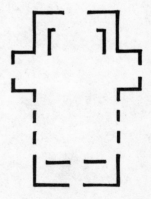

It is said that sailors would overturn their boats on a beach to protect themselves from sun or bad weather during a service of Christian worship and the arching roof of the church resembled this.

There is an accepted symbolism of form in church architecture in addition to a possible cruciform construction of the building as a whole.

The pointed arches common to Gothic churches and the pointed steeple of the New England churches both recall hands raised to God in prayer.

The number of panels in doors and windows have meaning too: two such panels stand for the Old and New Testaments; three, for the Trinity; four, for the Evangelists—Matthew, Mark, Luke, and John; five, for Christ and the Evangelists. The use of red paint for church doors—a growing custom—indicates that we enter into the church through the sacrificial blood of Christ.

The narthex or vestibule originally stood for "the world" and was a place for noncommunicants and penitents—not merely for late-comers! This makes the original placement of the baptismal font quite meaningful. (See page 33.)

The center aisle then becomes the life course of man until he comes face to face with God (at the chancel); *the pews* are the abode of the saints (members) and, if there are *pillars,* they stand for the apostles and so are twelve in number.

A cross when part of the chancel design, must be above all heads and all flags.

Usually, there are also reminders of great truths in Biblical words to be found in a church building—on the baptismal font and Communion table, over the chancel arch and doorways—sometimes even on the bells that call us to worship, for "blessed is the people that know the joyful sound" (Ps. 89:15).

The minister's robe is that of the Geneva scholar, and serves to emphasize his office rather than himself.

The choir, expressing the congregation's praise to God, should not be in evidence as persons. Positions at the side of the chancel or in the back gallery of the church, and the wearing of choir robes help to keep their part in the service unobtrusive.

Church Equipment

Without going into great detail some of the commonly accepted traditions are in regard to:

The pulpit, which in the Reformed churches is often in the center of the chancel, having the pulpit Bible as a focal point. Here the Word is read and proclaimed.

In some churches the lectern (reading desk) and pulpit are divided, on opposite sides of the chancel. As the minister reads Scripture or prays he is speaking for or to God; from the pulpit he interprets God's Word as a prophet.

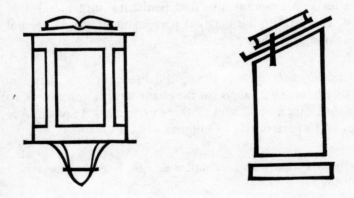

The Communion table, which should be on the level of the congregation in front of the pulpit, or between pulpit and lectern.

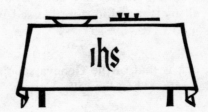

The baptismal font, which is often near the pulpit. Originally it was just inside the entrance of the church as a symbol that it is by baptism that we become part of the membership of Christ's church. A symbol of baptism has been the escalop shell with three drops of water, indicating that baptism was in the name of Father, Son, and Holy Spirit.

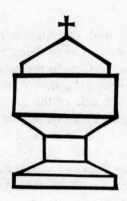

The Christian Flag

In September, 1897, the failure of a speaker to appear made it possible for Mr. Charles C. Overton, the church school superintendent, to share with his hearers an idea that came to him as he noticed the American flag draped over a corner of the pulpit (a very *wrong* use of the flag!). Drawing on his imagination, he described a Christian flag that would remind men of their allegiance to God as the national flag reminds them of their allegiance to their country.

During the week Mr. Overton had such a flag made, ready to use the following Sunday, and later he secured the interest and co-operation of a New York flag manufacturer. The use of the flag spread widely, since it is not restricted by national boundaries, but is equally significant anywhere in the world. It has no connection with warfare, but is the banner of the Prince of Peace, indicating allegiance only to the Kingdom of God. Numbers 2:3, which speaks of the "standard of the camp of Judah" as moving out at the head of Israel, is perhaps the precedent of a banner for the people of God. The colors blue and scarlet and white were also much used in the trappings of the Tabernacle.

It was eleven years later that a salute to the Christian flag was adopted for general use.

"I pledge allegiance to the Christian flag and to the Savior for whose kingdom it stands—one brotherhood, uniting all mankind in service and love."

Use of the Flags

Many churches display both the American and Christian flags in the church. Therefore questions as to their proper use are frequently raised. The following are the facts in the case:

The Federal Government asks that when the American flag is displayed it be on the right side of the group on the floor level on which the flag is displayed. This means that if a flag is on a stand, the base of which is on the floor level of the congregation or any assembly of people, it is supposed to be on the right side of that church. If it is on the floor level of a speaker or leader, and that floor level is above the floor level of the general group, the American flag should be on the right of that speaker.

This means that according to Government regulations, a flag displayed in any way on the chancel level of the church should be on the right of the minister, which would be the left of the congregation.

In using both the American and Christian flags, the situation is complicated by the fact that the General Assembly has taken action that the Christian flag should be "on the right"—there is no distinction made as to floor level.

One distinction that has been made in church schools when flag salutes are given has been to obey the Government regulation and have the American flag on the right and the Christian flag on the left. This was accepted because in the salute to the Christian flag the hand is put on the heart, and a symbolic connection was made in that way.

We feel it is right to state this case, leaving it to each individual user of flags as to the observances they want to follow. The simplest way to meet both regulations is to display the flags on a higher level than the general group, in which case Government regulations are observed and also General Assembly's pronouncement—for when you do this the Christian flag is on the right of the general group (with no regard for floor level) and the Government regulations are obeyed, due to the fact that the American flag is on the right of the leader at the floor level on which he stands.

We should not make such symbolism too complicated. We can, however, see that what symbols there are in the church in which we worship remind us of certain great truths in our faith or facts concerning the origin of the church. If a particular church is rich in symbolism, there should be careful records kept of every detail so that it can be constantly reinterpreted to children and young people and to new members of the congregation.

The Symbolism of Color

A somewhat less authentic but interesting symbolism is that of color. The traditional uses of it are somewhat arbitrary, but certain color-meanings have become generally accepted and are used in Christian art, in the designing of stained-glass windows, in the costuming of religious plays and pageants.

Paraments—that is, pulpit and lectern scarves, Communion table "runners," and pulpit Bible markers in colors symbolic of the seasons of the church year—are used in some churches. They are sometimes embroidered with the IHS, the Latin cross, the cross and crown, or the Celtic cross.

White—(the sum of all colors) is used for the festivals of our Lord, particularly that of the resurrection (Easter). It represents light, purity.

Red—(crimson) stands for our Lord's Passion, sacrificial love, Pentecost.

Green—means new or renewed life, the Trinity.

Purple—(violet) is used for the kingly aspect of our Lord, for Advent and Lent, for penitence.

Black—is the color of mourning, of Good Friday, of sin (the absence of light).

Gold—represents the wisdom of God. In the golden lights of a church building it brings *down* the wisdom of God to man, just as the arching roof indicates man's reaching toward God.

Orange—is the color of hearth and home, of the plenteous gifts for which we give thanks to God.

Brown—represents service to God and man—the color of the robe of Francis of Assisi. Red-brown means service offered in love.

Blue—stands for truth, constancy, faithfulness.

In *The Laws of Fesolé,* Ruskin says: "You will find the standard of color I am going to give you a safe one—the morning sky. The white, blue, purple, gold, scarlet, and ruby of morning clouds are meant to be entirely delightful to the human creatures whom the clouds and light sustain."

The Symbolism of the Church Year

There is another form of symbolism that has been neglected or forgotten by many Protestant churches—the symbolism of the church year. Traditionally, this special "calendar" has been associated also with color symbolism. The seasons of the church year and the colors associated with them are as follows:

Advent

Advent begins on the Sunday nearest November 30. The Alpha and Omega (see above) is the symbol of the Advent season, and violet, for thoughtfulness and penitence, its color. The message of Advent is, "Repent! and prepare for Christ's coming."

Christmastide

Christmastide extends from Christmas Eve (December 24) to Epiphany (January 6). Its symbol is IHS and its color, white—that which is used for all seasons closely connected with Christ. Its message is one of rejoicing.

Epiphany

Epiphany, January 6, the "twelfth night" after Christmas. Its symbol is the star, as it celebrates the visit of the Wise Men to the child Jesus—and therefore the star manifests Christ's coming to the Gentiles also. The color for Christmastide (white) continues until the last four days when the green of new life and hope is used. Epiphany calls us to show forth Christ's coming in word and deed, as the Wise Men followed the star.

Lent

Lent begins with Ash Wednesday, forty days before Holy Week. It is therefore not a fixed date. The color is the violet of penitence, and its message is: "Repent of your neglect of and indifference to the things of God. Live close to him and so renew your faith." (See below for its symbol.)

Christ's Passion

Christ's Passion includes the events of Holy Week. Its color is red, except for Friday, which is black; its note is of doom and sorrow. The cross is a symbol used from Ash Wednesday through Easter; the cross with the figure upon it symbolizes the crucifixion; an empty cross, the resurrection.

Easter

Easter is not a fixed date but is determined by the vernal equinox. The circle is sometimes used as a symbol of God's eternal power over death. White is the symbolic color, and the message of Easter is, "Rejoice! for now is Christ risen from the dead."

Ascension

Ascension is Thursday, forty days after Easter. Its symbol is the crown of Christ's victorious kingship; its color, white. It speaks to us of the hope of eternal life with God.

Pentecost

Pentecost or Whitsuntide, is the seventh Sunday after Easter. Its symbols are the dove and tongues of flame that symbolize the Holy Spirit. Red is the color, and the message "Witness!"

Trinity

Trinity extends from Pentecost to Advent. Its symbol is the triangle or trefoil (see above) and its color the green of renewal. Trinity says to us, "Now in fellowship with God the Father, Son and Holy Spirit, live as a child of God."

It is evident that a consciousness of this cycle of the Christian year could be to us a constant, symbolic reminder of the deepest and richest elements of our faith.

IV

THE USE OF SYMBOLISM
WITH CHILDREN

In the life of a particular church, the constant reinterpretation of symbols is a most important part of Christian nurture. As did the people of Israel, we lack words with enough scope and vigor, color and magnificence to express what God has done and is doing for us. And yet when we put our knowledge, our thoughts, and our feelings into other forms of communication we still have before us the task of helping the "listener" to understand what we are trying to say through symbols of many kinds.

To make use of symbolism in the church's task of Christian nurture there must be an understanding of the various ways in which, and the degrees to which, this kind of knowledge can play a useful part. Certainly first in this list should be the purpose of the Middle Ages—to "hear" the church speak the truths of God. This would mean a general understanding by all adults (particularly those who deal with children and youth) of whatever symbolism exists in the sanctuary. If there is a certain amount of symbolism used in other parts of the church building, inside or out, this should be a matter of available records secured from the architect, the designer of windows, and so on. Many churches put this kind of information into printed form when a building, a new window, or some equipment of a symbolic nature is dedicated, and file copies of such information should be readily available.

To this basic knowledge should be added a general understanding of symbolism so that the symbolic nature of certain materials, procedures, and acts is recognized, and the need for constant reinterpretation appreciated. How to use this knowledge in the plans for Christian nurture at each age level can then be considered.

Symbolism for the Very Young Child

As in all teaching, there must be an understanding of what the learner can grasp. The very young child may be able to apply a visible symbol to a specific person, object, or act—but hardly to a complex idea or concept; he would have trouble also with symbolic words, since his vocabulary is limited and a bit uncertain. In other words, he can learn that a green light means "cross the street" when "Onward, Christian Soldiers" is just an exciting but incomprehensible series of sounds.

In preschool groups one of the common uses of symbolism is that of a chosen sticker—a flower or animal—to mark the place where a particular child hangs his coat, his hat, and so on. The same marker is put inside boots, overshoes, and other personal possessions or work materials. On the surface, this appears to be entirely functional and otherwise meaningless. But it becomes, to the child, a symbol of himself. He objects in no uncertain terms to encroachments upon it without his permission. He learns to respect the "marks" of other children, thus avoiding endless arguments and quarrels.

As he paints, draws, or models in clay, this symbol becomes the mark of the creative artist, as real as a signature until he learns to print his name. To identify the similarly formless efforts of children as they experiment with materials of many kinds is not easy even for themselves! But they readily learn to put their "mark" on a completed easel painting, crayon drawing, or pot of planted seeds, before it is put aside for other activities.

Another mark of identification that a very young child can understand has to do with his offering envelope. A child is fascinated by the discovery that the number on the corner of the envelope is his number, that it is written in a big record book together with his name, and that in the book are entered his gifts for the work of the church. In a church that uses the Youth Budget, the church school or church treasurer can bring the big book into the kindergarten and both show and explain this process—at the same time adding meaning to the process by telling of some of the ways the money is used.

One clever teacher of very young children found a way to "symbolize" changes of activity for the group without saying a word. On an easel within the sight of all, she would put certain pictures signifying the time for such changes—a carefully chosen picture of children singing ("come to the piano"); of a group listening to a story ("come, gather together"); of children at work around a table ("now we have work to do"); of rest with eyes closed and heads on a table, or stretched out on a mat ("now let us be very quiet"); putting on wraps ("it's time to get ready to go home"). As with the Scout's "silence signal" of the lifted hand and arm, one child sees and responds, and the response spreads. A gradual shift from one interest to another is made without signaling by any kind of sound.

Of course, sounds can be used in the same way—not the sharp, sudden sound of a bell or a loud voice, but a familiar strain of music, with or without words. It can be hummed or sung as a teacher moves about the room and will often be echoed by the children themselves. It can be played on a piano, autoharp, harmonica, or xylophone. Whatever form it takes—and of course, always the same form—the music becomes a symbol of change to a new interest or activity, or to the quiet times of relative inactivity.

The teacher's Bible, placed at hand for ready use, can become a very real symbol of the Word of God, without use of that somewhat abstract phrase.

"The story is in our Bible [open in the teacher's hands]. It is one God wanted us to hear and think about."

"Jesus said these words; God sent him to tell us how important they are."

"David was a shepherd, long, long ago. There are stories about him in the Bible. He said words like these when he thanked God for his love and care."

Through such simple phrases used with sincerity and understanding, a child begins to understand this particular Book to be God's Word to all of us, and to feel something of its importance to the adults who mean so much to him in church and home. If the teacher uses her own Bible and tells when and how it became her own, this is another way of stressing the symbolism.

Even with this age group there must be some contact with the symbolism of the place of congregational worship. This can be done in either of two ways. One is to select in advance a few symbols in the sanctuary to tell about as a small group of children visit there. Another and much more difficult way to proceed is to tell the group to look at everything carefully as you walk around the sanctuary and to ask if there is anything about which they want to know more. This procedure calls for some careful "homework" on the part of the teacher. She must not only be familiar with the uses and meanings of practically everything in the sanctuary, but she must have ready some brief and simple *words* of explanation, for there is no way to predict what will interest a child.

It is important here to carefully avoid any lengthy or detailed statements and to try very hard to put the explanation in terms that have meaning to the group. For instance, having become accustomed to the frequent use of and reference to the Bible, the children will be interested in the pulpit Bible. A new aspect is added to their conception of the Bible as God's Word if they are told, "Mr. . . . . [the minister] uses the Bible to read to your mommies and daddies what God wants them to know; and then he helps them to understand what it means, and what God wants them to do."

Let us suppose that in a given church somewhere, in some form there appear the symbols basic to the Reformed faith and, of course, to the Biblical record. It is comforting to know how little the small child wants to know about symbols ("pictures") that attract or are called to his attention!

Suppose we consider first the symbol of the fish, and those symbolic words Jesus applied to himself together with the Chi Rho and IHS and the Alpha and Omega (see Chapter II). They can be explained to the very young child as follows:

"The people who knew and loved Jesus remembered everything he said and did. They made pictures and words to remind them of the wise words he spoke and the loving acts he did. This is one of them."

In the case of the lamb, the cup, the bread, the door, the light (candle or lamp), something more might be added, especially for the five-year-olds.

"The lamb reminded people that Jesus cared about them as a good shepherd did for his sheep."

"Listening to Jesus tell about God's love was, to the people, like having a cool drink of water when we are very thirsty, or a piece of bread when we are very hungry. What he said made them feel ever so much better."

"There was no one that people wanted to see more than Jesus. He was always a welcome guest—the one they opened the door for gladly."

"Having Jesus come to see them or talk to them was like having a light turned on in a dark room. They could see everything better because he was there."

The children will, of course, not understand fully such words. But if they are said with sincerity, a *feeling* about their meaning, and the importance of Jesus to people who knew him, and to the speaker —someone they know and love *now*—will stay with some of them.

The cross—including the anchor—the pelican, and the symbols of the crucifixion should neither be evaded nor emphasized. If you prefer, they can be included in the "reminders" of Jesus. Or it is possible to say something of this kind:

"Everyone did not love Jesus. The people who did not, killed him in a very cruel way. His friends used this (the cross) and other pictures to remind them that Jesus loved even the people who hated and hurt him. He asked God to forgive them."

The good shepherd symbol is quite common and can be explained somewhat as follows: "Many of the people who knew Jesus had their own sheep and took good care of them. They found green grass and cool water for the sheep; they cleared sharp stones away from their path. The shepherd protected them from wild animals too—bears and lions and snakes. At night they rubbed bruises and sore places with oil and took thorns and burrs from their woolly coats.

"These people knew that Jesus loved and cared for them just as much as the shepherd did for his sheep. And Jesus told them God cares for all people the same way too."

The stories mentioned as symbols of the resurrection should not be used with preschool children in that way. If used, they should be simply in direct story form, as people God took care of for special— and unspecified—reasons.

The Trinity is difficult enough for adults and can hardly be explained to little children. Therefore the symbols of the Trinity can be explained as picture-words for God. An attempt might possibly be made to speak of the Trinity in terms of "God; and Jesus whom God sent to us; and God's voice, speaking to us in many ways." But even this presents serious problems and dangers. The usual symbol of God, the hand, can be briefly explained as a picture-word that reminds us of all the wonderful things God has done for us and of his many gifts.

If there is one stained-glass window that has a story familiar to them, this can be pointed out and the related words read from the Bible. If a figure of Jesus is the only familiar object, this can be added to the growing number of pictures of Jesus they have seen, with the usual comment, "This is a picture of the way the artist (or the maker of the window) liked to imagine Jesus." For, of course, our representations of Jesus in art are, in a very real sense, symbolic rather than actual. Complex or unfamiliar picture windows can be explained by saying, "That is another story you will hear someday."

The symbols of the church, of the church year, and of color are not apt to be noticed by children of this age, nor is it advisable to call attention to them. Possible exceptions might be the vine, the Christian flag, the pulpit and lectern, the Communion table and baptismal font. The latter two should be pointed out if they are not noticed and explained in terms such as those indicated above.

The vine will be noticed by children because its form is familiar to them. One might say:

"Do you remember (or see) how thick and close to the vine the leaves and bunches of grapes grow? Jesus told the people that everyone must be that close to God, so they can know what he wants them to do."

Any simple version of the story of the Christian flag could be told. But it would seem wise to say merely: "That is the flag of the church. It reminds us how much we love our church, just as the Stars and Stripes remind us of how much we love our country." If questions have been asked and answered about the cross, the form of it on the flag might be mentioned, but this is not necessary.

The pulpit can be explained as "the place where the minister stands when he tells the people what God wants them to do"; and the lectern, "the place where the minister stands when he reads the Bible or prays to God."

There are, in the preschool groups, certain acts that are symbolic. One has been the lighting of birthday candles. But there can be a better celebration of such events in song, poem, prayer, or ritual, by which the wonder of learning and growing is stressed.

Another is the giving of an offering. No matter when, where, or how the gifts are received, it is necessary to constantly reinterpret the meaning and purposes of such gifts. Kindergarten children can understand that when we give to the work of the church our gifts are tokens of our gratitude to God for his much greater gifts to us. They can also be helped to understand what the money does, in part, for the particular church and for the work of that church in our country and overseas, if this is done in terms of specific needs—oil for heating, brooms for cleaning, and educational supplies, food, and medicine. Such content added to this symbolic act may be greatly reinforced if parents help to interpret it also.

A small child is deeply interested in baptism, another symbolic act. The children should see the celebration of this sacrament, especially if it concerns a member of their family. In the simplest way they can be told of their own baptism (if infant baptism is the custom of the church) and something of the love and concern for the baptized child that parents and congregation express in this way.

It is even possible to have at least the older kindergarten children know something of the meaning of the Communion service— another symbolic act. Perhaps a few of the children can see its celebration or visit the church as the elders prepare for such a service. This can be explained somewhat as follows: "Before Jesus left his friends he had supper with them. As they ate together he took bread, like this, and a cup of wine, like this. He told them to remember him every time they ate the bread or drank from the cup. When your mommies and daddies take this bread and wine they too remember Jesus, how he loves them and how they love him."

In all these ways a beginning is made in the understanding of symbolism long before the word is heard or used. The children's passing interest in what they see and hear is not apt to stay with them; nor will the explanations necessarily be remembered. But as such experiences are renewed and expanded in upper departments, there may be a vague sense of familiarity and, in some cases, a more vivid interest because of partial memories. And the feeling of being a part of something that is important to those adults they love and trust will remain, and is worth all the time and effort.

Symbolism for the Primary Child

As a child grows and learns, certain symbols are discarded and others take their place. He learns to read and write his name, and prefers to use this written name to identify his possessions rather than to use a decorative sticker. Thus, he is quite familiar with symbols, for they are all around him in the community of which he is increasingly a part.

Pictures or objects in a primary group can be used as symbols of a line of words in a hymn, a poem, or a Bible passage being memorized. Since primary children as a rule still do not read quickly and easily, materials to be used in worship must be memorized. The pictures or objects that help in this process may even be made by the children themselves, but in use they become a reminding symbol of a group of words.

For instance, a hymn-poem such as "All Things Bright and Beautiful" can be learned very quickly by using a series of pictures to symbolize successive phrases. Or, a diorama or tabletop scene of a shepherd caring for his sheep among the hills of Palestine can be used as a reminding aid in learning Ps. 23—which in itself is a symbol in words of God's sustaining love.

In one church a primary group gathered for a church-wide hunt for a symbol known to be used quite frequently throughout the building. They had been having the few stories there are of Jesus' early life, and had heard, discussed, and learned Luke 2:52, "And Jesus increased in wisdom and in stature, and in favor with God and man." They learned that a symbol something like a four-leaf clover is used in churches and by several organizations for children to "stand for" four ways people can grow. They themselves made such a design in colored medallions like a stained-glass window and agreed on a wording for its meaning—"We grow in our bodies, we learn things with our minds, we learn how to get along with people, and we try more and more to show our love for God."

Of course, the teachers of the group had looked for the symbol in advance, and had found it in twenty-nine places; but in less than an hour the primary children had found it in thirty-two! This hunt became a tradition with each completely new group in the department, and the symbol, the verse, and a related song, "Glad I Am to Grow!" became a part of the celebration of each child's birthday.

A symbolic *act* in which the primary children shared in one church was the taking up of the first few shovels of earth when the cornerstone of a new building was laid, "because this building is for our children, and our children's children."

Even more than in the kindergarten, the primary children should become acquainted with understandable symbols in the sanctuary and with the symbolic acts of the worshiping congregation. They can see a baptismal service and the celebration of the Lord's Supper and will be interested in the preparation for these events, and in the way the minister and an elder take Communion to those who are shut-in or ill.

As with the preschool children, the primary child is interested in the baptismal service because of the way in which it is part of his life. When this matter is presented in the curriculum, or when the children visit the sanctuary and see the baptismal font, several helpful suggestions can be made.

For instance, a mimeographed sheet explaining what is to happen might be sent to the parents, asking them to show their child his baptismal certificate and tell him something of where, when, and how his baptism took place. An addition to this would be a note from the minister, reminding parents that the baptismal service is not the giving of a name, but a mark of God's acceptance of their child into the Christian community. He might also remind them of the responsibility for Christian nurture undertaken by them and by the congregation in behalf of the child. When there is an excursion into the *empty* sanctuary, the sacrament of Baptism, and the uses of the pulpit, lectern, and pulpit Bible might well be explained by the minister.

Sometimes it is well to ask an elder and his wife to explain—and show—the preparation for the Lord's Supper, including a brief reference to the preparatory service. If such friends are not accustomed to small children, the necessary brevity and simplicity must be carefully discussed in advance. At the same time the kit used by the minister and an elder in taking Communion with shut-ins can be displayed and explained, as can something of the meaning and procedure in the service itself.

Remember to stress the fact that this teaching experience should not aimed at detailed explanation of either procedure or meaning, but that the basic purpose should be to make clear the *importance* of this Sacrament to Christians.

To younger primary children the use of the symbols connected with Jesus Christ must be handled with the same brevity and simplicity as was suggested for preschool children, with certain additions for older primary children, such as:

The fish—in the primary year on The Church, the children learn of the persecution faced by the early Christians. They can therefore understand the need for a secret sign of recognition of one another and for places of meeting.

The "I am" symbols can be connected with the words Jesus said about himself, such as:
"I am the true vine" (John 15:1–2).
"I am the good shepherd" (John 10:11).
"Whoever drinks of the water that I shall give him will never thirst" (John 4:14).
"I am the bread of life" (John 6:48).
"I am the door" (John 10:9).
"I am the light of the world" (John 8:12).

Since many third-grade primary groups are beginning to learn how to use a Bible, these words can be read to them as the symbols are seen and the above simple explanations of them are given.

More also can be done about the symbols of the crucifixion, for primary children hear this story in some detail. However, they should be, to this child, just picture-reminders of the way Jesus died. One's explanation of the cross must be made from a combination of convictions about its meaning and what one believes about the understanding of children of this age. Taking into account some of the meanings taught in this age group, it should be entirely possible to say something like this:

"As you know, some people hated Jesus and did not want to accept what he taught. So they killed him on a cross, as wicked men were killed in those days. Jesus could have avoided this, but he did not, for it was part of what God sent him to do. All through the years God's people had forgotten his care for them, and failed to return his love. Again and again they failed to trust and obey him, even though his love was shown in the Creation, in many mighty acts, in words he spoke to them himself or through chosen messengers. There was nothing left to do but to come to earth in Jesus Christ and in him show by word and deed that his love was great enough to last *no matter what men did to him.*

"So Jesus did not fight back when men killed him.

[NOTE: Do not use wording that lays the blame for Jesus' death on any person or group. He died of the arrogance, pride, and self-will of men, in which we share.]

"But when Jesus came back to life in the resurrection, men began to see that God's love was stronger than anything, even death."

Do not use the Bible stories thought of as symbolic of the resurrection with primary children. It is better for them, as for the pre-schoolers, to take such stories as evidence of God's sustaining care of his people at special times, and for particular reasons.

The symbol for God can be understood in much the same terms as in the kindergarten, but more can be done with the Trinity *after* the primary children have had the Pentecost story in their study of the church. You might say:

"When people tried to explain God or to name him they had as much trouble as they had in Moses' time. There was the creating, sustaining God who made and cares for all things, who is everywhere and forever. There is God as he came to earth in Jesus, whom men could see and know, as loving and forgiving. And when Jesus finally went away, he promised that God's Spirit would be with his people. Knowing God in three ways and yet knowing he was one and the same, men used the word 'trinity' or 'three in one' to show that they knew God as the Father, the Son (Jesus), and the Holy Spirit. This is hard for grownups to understand even though they *believe* it—so it will be hard for you."

It is in the proper framework of session plans that the symbols of the Trinity, together and apart, may be used. The church symbols are still difficult at this age, except for further or repeated explanation of those used with the preschool children. The words of the salute to the Christian flag might be memorized, although this is not necessary. Because primary children are interested in words, any that are carved or painted within the church might be found, read, and explained. Such words, usually Biblical, are commonly found on the Communion table and the baptismal font, or over the chancel arch or entrance door.

The Bible stories told to primary children will contain many

references to symbols, the meaning of which must be made clear—
a rainbow, a pillar of cloud and fire, the ark, symbols of God's promises and of his continuing presence with his people.

One primary department, after a conference with the church
treasurer, prepared an exhibit of objects symbolizing the various
ways in which the church made use of the money gifts of its people.
Curriculum materials and supplies, heat and light, staff and building maintenance, all could be found in symbols, together with a globe
marking the church's world-wide service. This became an interesting
part of the Every Member Canvass, as well as a worth-while bit of
learning for the children.

All this indicates a fact to be remembered: for the primary child,
symbols must still be simple, direct, concrete, even though there can
be more of them. His interest in them is not conceptual, but centers
in use.

Symbolism for the Junior

A new element in symbolism for the junior issues in symbolized
knowledge. The way in which Bible references are written has an
element of symbolism. As he learns to use the hymnal, he finds in
the metrical signature under the name of the hymn a new kind of
symbol, and one that gives him some choice in the use of tunes. The
meanings underlying Biblical phrases he finds painted or carved in
the church and other public buildings, or quoted in books, in maga-
zines, and in newspapers, begin to interest him.

Now the symbolism of the church building, its order of service,
its sacramental acts, can be shared in all their richness.

There is no limit to a junior's understanding of the symbols of
our Reformed faith, as the Biblical material is all being opened up
to him. At this age, however, a single excursion into the church
sanctuary is not the best approach. Rather, the symbols should be
found and studied as they become relevant to the curriculum. All
the symbols for Jesus Christ can be related to a study of his life and
teachings at appropriate times. The Passion symbols become especially meaningful as does the cross. It is possible to go into more of
the some four hundred types of crosses that have been designed and
made through the ages, the stories of their origins, and their varying
shades of meaning. However, this hardly seems worth-while in most

instances. For the few juniors deeply interested a book on the subject, well written and illustrated, might be added to your reference library or borrowed for a short time.

For this age, the symbolic implication given to certain Old Testament stories will have real interest. Older juniors will enjoy comparing their meaning in the Biblical epic with this special interpretation of them. They might, in this connection, find photographs of the crude illustrations of these stories found in the catacombs and other meeting places of the early Christians.

The symbols of the Trinity—apart and together—can be used more extensively than with primary children, although the basic teaching about them would be much the same.

It is, however, at the point of symbolism of the church—its meaning, history, and architecture—that much new teaching can be done. This is possible both because of much more knowledge concerning the church, but also because juniors are—or should be—attending congregational worship. Everything possible should be done to deepen their interest and participation in it.

Juniors should be familiar with the calendar of the church year and the paraments that mark its progress. They might indeed work to purchase the latter if their church does not possess them—or even to make a set if there is adult leadership available that can guide such a process to a skillful and effective conclusion.

Juniors can now begin to recognize the symbolism of line and wood carving in their own and other churches. In fact, if their particular church has little of such symbolism, the boys and girls should have guided tours to several churches that do, including a Jewish synagogue. They can study the records of their own church for information about its symbolism and make this available for study by other groups, in the form of slides made by color photography, by drawings of their own, in a carefully made book of the data collected, or by any number of similar processes. They should be reminded (or informed) even more fully concerning the symbolic acts of baptism and the Lord's Supper, studying the words of the two services in their own denomination's service book. An earnest junior, feeling that he meets the conditions of the invitation extended, may ask why he cannot take Communion. This is an opportunity to recall the promises made in his behalf by parents and congregation (in churches that practice infant baptism), each sharing in nurturing him to the point at which a public confession of faith puts responsibility on his own shoulders and admits him to the Lord's Supper. Of course, in churches in which adult baptism only is practiced, teaching leading up to baptism is vital. The parallel in the Jewish faith of becoming a "Son of the Law" in the ceremonies of *bar mitzvah* is interesting to know about and to experience at this age. Also the visit of Jesus to the Temple at twelve years takes on new meaning.

The symbolic words and acts and the order of the service of congregational worship should be explained at this age, especially to sixth-graders. This material can be presented in chart form, telling what is happening in the service, the meaning of each procedure, and how the worshiper should participate. An example of such a chart may be found at the end of this chapter.

Color symbolism, especially that of the church year, can be a very real interest to some juniors. Interest in color as a part of Christian drama comes at a later period but can be carefully studied in the making of stained-glass designs. The Christian flag can be seen in this context also.

Juniors love to reproduce symbols in a wide variety of media for use in their own, or their church school, rooms. Many objects decorated with symbols can be used in worship, such as offering plates and wall hangings that are designed to follow the course of the church year. Or they can be made into symbolic designs in block prints for greeting cards, for programs, for the covers made for their booklets for personal devotions, or for furnishings and equipment in the junior department. Juniors across the country have themselves reproduced Christian symbols in beaten copper and silver, in glass and modeling clay, in oils and pastels.

In one church, juniors serve as the guides to conduct small groups of visitors or new members on tours around the church building, explaining its symbolism. The sixth-grade class made a series of colored slides (such as have been mentioned) to project as an aid in this process. In another, the boys and girls designed and made medallions of simulated stained glass for the centers of a series of windows on the side of a long, dull corridor. The medallions included traditional symbols of the church in history and around the world, with a few designed to represent historic events in their own church.

A junior contribution to the preparation for an Every Member Canvass was dramatically symbolic. From information published in Washington the group worked out proportionately the amount of money spent in this country for such popular items as cars and liquor, chewing gum and cosmetics, tobacco and movies. Representing these figures in lengths of bright ribbons proved quite an eye opener, for while some of those which stood for the items named reached the length of the center aisle once or more, "interfaith benevolences" reached just a short distance from the pulpit, and the ribbon representing denominational benevolences could hardly be seen at all.

Juniors are beginning to study as well as to enjoy some of the art forms of the church other than architecture, that are symbolic wholly or in part. Many great paintings have details rooted in symbolism—details often so "hidden" that a junior who discovers them has a real sense of satisfaction. Similar discoveries can be made in various crafts of the church—metal work, tapestries, carved wood, bas-reliefs, statues. Where actual contact with such art forms is not possible, good reproductions of some of them can be found in local or state libraries or through the extension departments of museums.

Some use has been made with juniors of forms of the early mystery and morality plays, which in characterization, costuming, and language contain a great deal of symbolism that is understandable to juniors. The symbolism of hymns is interesting to them also, and illustrating these vivid phrases is one way of memorizing them. Although they can understand such symbolic words they do not often create them, as their own forms of verbal communication are usually concrete.

Of course, much of symbolism on the level of children is representative, rather than subtly meaningful. But they are learning a language, a kind of artistic shorthand of representation. And a great deal of it does—and more could—have real meaning and value in a clearer and deeper perception of the things of our faith. Those who grow up blind and deaf to symbolic expression will surely miss a large part of life and religion.

A Chart: THE CHURCH SERVICE

ORDER OF SERVICE	PURPOSE	WHAT I MAY DO
SILENT PRAYER	Ask God's blessing on the pastor, people, and one's self.	Bow my head; ask God to bless my pastor, the people, and our worship together.
PRELUDE	Help people to become quiet and conscious of God's nearness.	Enjoy the music; think about God's goodness.
CALL TO WORSHIP	Bring all the people together in a thought of God.	Follow the words carefully; think what they mean to me.
INVOCATION	Unite all people in a prayer for God's blessing on their worship.	Bow my head; think of the words and thoughts as the minister speaks.
HYMNS	Express in words and music the praise, desires, and feelings of the people.	Think of each word; sing as if the hymns were written to express my own thoughts and feelings.
SCRIPTURE	Hear God speak to us and reveal himself through the Bible.	Listen carefully; try to understand what is read.
PASTORAL PRAYER	Bring the people before God: their love for him; their thanks, confessions, petitions.	Listen to the minister's words; try to feel that everyone is praying them; add my own words.
ANTHEM OR SOLO	Express feeling as well as thought through music.	Try to understand and think of the words of the singer; feel the music, and enjoy it.
OFFERING	Give to others because of our love for God.	Say thank you to God as my gift is given—no matter how small it may be.
OFFERTORY AND PRAYER	Help people to feel thankful to God in a spirit of worship.	Enjoy the music; continue to think of God's goodness.
SERMON	Help people to understand what God says to them in the Bible—what he wants us to be and do.	Listen for the Scripture called the "text." Try to find one thing meant for me.

ORDER OF SERVICE	PURPOSE	WHAT I MAY DO
BENEDICTION	Give God's blessing to the people.	Bow my head; give thanks that God will be with me through the week and always.
POSTLUDE	Express through music the joy and purpose for life found in the service of worship.	Sometimes sit quietly and listen to it. Notice that it is joyous and purposeful.
FELLOWSHIP AT THE CLOSE OF THE SERVICE	Welcome strangers, enjoy friends, because we are all members of God's family.	Say "good morning" to friends and strangers because I am a part of the church.

V

THE USE OF SYMBOLISM
WITH YOUTH AND ADULTS

Symbolism for Young People

It is in the youth group that symbolism comes into its own as a way of expressing ideas, concepts, ideals. An expanded vocabulary and a background of experience that is wider and deeper both contribute to this.

If the groundwork of an understanding of the symbols of the Christian faith has been laid, as they are presented in the first two chapters of this book, even the task of preparing young people for communicant membership in the church becomes easier. As they begin to take a real part in the life and worship of the congregation, their world of symbols expands, as does their ability to communicate in symbols.

By this time they should have a thorough acquaintance with the symbolism of a church with which they have been connected since childhood, so that it constantly "speaks" to them of their faith. If they move from church to church, there should be a sufficient interest in these matters to arouse curiosity about anything new they see.

There is, of course, no necessity to omit or dilute for young people any of the meaning of the symbols described in this book. Everything mentioned should be a part of this knowledge. Leaders of youth need only check as to what has not previously been part of their knowledge and understanding and go on from there—or go back to fill up the gaps. The projects that interest juniors can be approached much more elaborately and creatively by youth.

One new experience can be of great value, as studies of comparative religions and of the differences between denominations are made. They all have a rich historical symbolism; but the younger churches are expressing religious concepts in their own terms. Modern architects too are finding ways to express religious ideas and ideals in art forms of functional simplicity and a new kind of clearcut beauty. All these developments can be studied by young people and adults with profit. Often such studies rid us of prejudices and misunderstandings when we realize that art forms and symbols that seem to us pagan stand for meanings that go far beyond what they appear to be.

At this point the stories behind the creation of art forms—mystery plays and cathedrals; highly symbolic paintings, both medieval and modern; tales of the creation of great church music, such as the oratorios—these and many others are of interest.

Young people, too, can understand and make full use of the symbolic use of color. One senior high group was asked to plan framing and settings for a number of very fine paintings given for use in certain class and department rooms in their church school. They finally agreed on a common background of wood paneling, painted in tones that would bring out the color values of each painting, with hidden lighting to emphasize details for study, and with velvet draw curtains to either cover or frame the picture. The hangings were of colors that had some symbolic meaning suitable for the use to which the room was being put.

In the same way young people can make use of the symbolism of color in drama—in backgrounds, properties, and costumes. This, if done well, can take the place of elaborate and realistic settings, centering instead on the mood of a scene and upon the actors.

The difficulty with youth may lie in the very fact of their wholehearted response to symbolism. Their worship services can become a series of rites, more aesthetic than meaningful, calling forth emotion rather than thoughtful consideration of truth. There may soon be candles and ceremonies, processionals and litanies all over the place!

Young people with special interests can be helped to make use of their hobbies to discover and express ideas in symbols. Many stamps and coins have a degree of religious symbolism. Our symbolic forms appear frequently in nature—as, for instance, in the fish skeleton found in Florida which forms a perfect crucifix.

In a certain church a group of junior highs both stimulated and satisfied a curiosity that eventually meant a great deal to the congregation. Certain sections of the stonework on the outside of the building ended in small figures in relief—the heads and shoulders of men. They were not conventional, but quite evidently portrait heads, each one different. A question asked in the junior high fellowship started a hunt for information about them. None was found in the church records; the architect was no longer available. One of the leaders suspected that they might be characters in church history and suggested some research along that line. Eventually all but two of the heads were identified, and the information obtained in doing so was put into a small booklet by the group for the official church records. It was even illustrated to prove their point—for while the portraits found in old books were not available, one of the boys got permission to photograph them and reproduce them as part of the book.

The interest in the arts that had a beginning with juniors also "springs full bloom" among youth. Established hobbies, developed talents, and vocational interests enter into the picture. Unfortunately, just as this happens, the church begins to depend almost entirely on words for communication of the faith to and by young people. Somehow it has come to be assumed that the creative activity so commonly used in younger groups is too childish a form of expression from now on.

But this is not true where young people and adults continue to advance both in skills and in the concepts to be expressed. Painting in oils or pastels, being an avocation of many famous men and women, has attained a certain respectability. But in the minds of most people, finger painting is for the kindergarten! One youth group, however, having in some way gotten over the hurdle of that impression, found finger painting a wonderful way to express some of the discussions they had been having about the events of Holy Week. The symbols they produced for each day of that week, both in color and beauty of line, were remarkable.

Another senior high group was given special responsibility by the church of which it was a part for the festival seasons of the church year. This included decorating the sanctuary for three such occasions, and the production of one pageant. With the help of an interested adviser, they studied the symbolic use of color and line in decoration, costuming, and settings. The result was outstanding.

A very real addition at this point, however—in spite of the emphasis so far on activity—is in the symbolic use of words. The language of our faith and of the Scriptures upon which it is based is very largely symbolic. This is what makes so much of the Bible difficult for children. But young people have begun to organize concrete experiences of childhood into abstract terms—to generalize. They have put their own meaning into such words as "faith," "love," "courage." And they are also able, with help, to find meaning in such words as "grace," "sin," "salvation," "mission."

Young people—and of course, children as well—are often in choirs. But it is at this stage of growth that the symbolic use of words in hymns and anthems should be carefully interpreted and their Biblical sources studied under the guidance of their director.

Words such as these should—and do—relate to a whole series of events, values, and understandings that go far beyond the basic meanings of the words themselves. But this happens only when the words have been illumined by the personal experience of the learner, by the shared experiences of others, and by the guidance and interpretation that helps the learner to understand both. Words, both oral and written, are a tool for young people as they seek to comprehend and express their faith. They appear in church school studies, in hymns and anthems, in sermons and Christian literature. The only way to be sure their symbolic meaning is understood is by means of constant reinterpretation.

Symbolism for Adults

All that has been said about the knowledge and use of symbolism and symbolic meanings in Christian education concerning children and youth is true of adults too. It is also true that unless those who deal with children *and* adults—parents, teachers, leaders—are interested in and informed about a simple, clear-cut, Biblically based symbolism, nothing that matters will happen to help them see and understand a whole world of meanings around them. Leaders need to be informed because only if they are, will it be possible for them to make a sharp distinction between the kind of symbolism described in the first two chapters of this book and the elaborate systems devised by artists, architects, and ecclesiastics. They need to be interested because only if they are will the necessary groundwork be laid and the necessary teaching done. This is not easy—in terms of study, planning—or legwork!

Probably what is in the first three chapters of this book is as much as many adults would want to know about symbolism. But this much they *should* know if they are in a teaching relationship (including that of parents) to children, young people, or adults who are growing in Christian knowledge and understanding. For in such a relationship there is the ever-present opportunity to awaken curiosity and interest, to open minds to new meanings, to illustrate truth in new ways. To do this it is important that a particular church make its own symbolism clear to its people and that this be repeated periodically and in detail. Suggestions have been made in previous chapters as to ways in which juniors and young people can help in doing this.

However, as in all good teaching, there are special values in the process for adults. One of these is obviously what was originally intended—that buildings erected for worship may speak in many ways of the faith proclaimed in them. This is an enriching experience. The walls around you, the art forms you see, the music and words you hear, are suddenly more meaningful, more colorful, and have more scope.

The list of references at the end of this book will enable those who are sufficiently interested to go much farther in the study of Biblically based and historical symbolism. Closely related to our own thinking in this area would be the symbolism of the Jewish religion, both in its architecture, and in the rituals of home and synagogue. There would be many meanings common to all Christians in the symbolism of the High-Church type—Roman, Greek Orthodox, Episcopalian, Lutheran. An interest in art would probably be necessary to lead anyone to follow through any real study of the highly complex symbolism of medieval times. The same interest might turn one to consideration of the symbolism of medieval or Renaissance paintings of Biblical subjects.

It would be of value to adults as well as to young people to study the symbolism of modern art forms expressing Christian concepts in architecture, in the graphic arts, in church equipment of all kinds. This would be especially true as church groups become better acquainted with the many ways in which ancient cultures are contributing to, and creating new forms of, Christian art and symbolism. In the younger churches of Africa, Asia, and Latin America, Christianity frequently adopted, but reinterpreted, the art forms and rituals of the pagan religions from which its people had been set free—and this same thing is still happening around the world.

If we really want the very walls of the particular church of which we are members to speak of our faith, we will consider this as plans are made for a new building, or for alterations in an old one. Frequently such studies, and the co-operation of a good architect, will enable building committees to save large amounts—by replacing traditional designs and materials with a functional simplicity and materials that do not call for so much expensive maintenance—and yet preserving the concept of a building that speaks of a faith.

Studies of this kind can be carried on by reading certain of the books listed in the Bibliography, by carefully planned visits to churches rich in various types of symbolism, and by exploring the resources of nearby museums of art. In an area in which such churches and museums are not available, church members who travel can use photographic equipment to take color slides that will be helpful. Also, many of the great museums sell or rent slides, films, and prints for such studies.

Adults will frequently be able to share the evidence of their hobbies to add to the understanding of symbolism in the church community. Photography has been mentioned; one way it can be useful is in taking color slides of projects connected with symbolism initiated by children or young people. In this way, a permanent record can be made of such projects without depriving individuals of the results of their efforts. Collections of stamps and coins, bells and wood carvings, tapestries and Oriental rugs not only are frequently highly symbolic, but their symbolism is often of a religious nature. The historical society of one denomination has an interesting collection of Communion tokens most of which—while crude—have a symbolic marking of some kind; besides, they are, in themselves, symbols of the necessity for preparing mind, heart, and life before partaking of the Lord's Supper.

It would be a new experience for most adults to attempt to express Christian concepts in art forms rather than in words—but it would surely be a most rewarding one. There is no end to the possibilities —one could weave or embroider, paint or model, act, sing, or dance such concepts, once self-consciousness and too deep a concern with excellence ceases to inhibit the free expression of beliefs and feelings.

But fundamentally the richest avenue of symbolic expression for adults is through the use of words. It is only as vocabulary expands, experiences broaden and deepen, and more detailed Biblical studies are engaged in that this can happen. There is a language of faith— a Biblical language—that must be learned with understanding and precision if our theology is to be soundly based. This language is highly abstract and symbolic, and yet lacking knowledge of it, we stumble into error both in our learning and in our witness. Sin and salvation, mission and commitment, the new life and the suffering servant are words with a world of meaning and experience bound up in them. To the nonbeliever they are as incomprehensible as "speaking with tongues." To the Christian adult they are—or should be— rich in content based on knowledge, understanding, and experience.

All the symbols of line and color, of object, art, and sound should remind us of the meanings in such words, for this must be their only purpose. To make sure that this is a reality is a teaching task that has no end.

BIBLIOGRAPHY

Symbols and Symbolism

Griffith, Helen Stuart, *The Sign Language of Our Faith.* Morehouse-Barlow Co., Inc., 1944.

Johnson, Frederich Ernest, *Religious Symbols.* Harper & Brothers, 1955.

McGee, Ratha Doyle, *Symbols: Signposts of Devotion.* The Upper Room, 1956.

Rest, Friedrich, *Our Christian Symbols.* Christian Education Press, 1954.

Stafford, Thomas Albert, *Christian Symbolism in the Evangelical Churches.* Abingdon Press, 1942.

Symbols in Various Art Forms

Lowrie, Walter, *Art in the Early Church.* Pantheon Books, Inc., 1947.

Maus, Cynthia Pearl, *The Church and the Fine Arts.* Harper & Brothers, 1960.

Ritter, Richard H., *The Arts of the Church.* The Pilgrim Press, 1947.

NOTE: A book that is out of print but exceedingly valuable, *The Goldsmith of Florence,* can be found in many public libraries, in the art reference section.

Symbols in Worship

Bays, Alice A., *Worship Programs in the Fine Arts.* Abingdon Press, 1940.

Lothrop, Florence Fitch, *One God—The Way We Worship Him.* Lothrop, Lee & Shepard Co., Inc., 1944.

Smith, Jean Louise, *Great Art and Children's Worship.* Abingdon Press, 1948.

Symbolism That Includes the Secular

Ferguson, George, *Signs and Symbols in Christian Art,* with illustrations from paintings of the Renaissance. Oxford University Press, 1954.

Koch, Rudolf, *The Book of Signs,* tr. by Vyvyan Holland. Dover Publications, Inc., 1955.

Lehner, Ernst, *The Picture Book of Symbols.* The Wm. Penn Publishing Corporation, 1956.

Lehner, Ernst, *Symbols, Signs and Signets.* The World Publishing Company, 1950.

Symbols in Projects

Barbour, Russell, and Barbour, Ruth, *Religious Ideas for Arts and Crafts.* Christian Education Press, 1959.

Symbols Around the World

Fleming, Daniel Johnson, *Christian Symbols in a World Community.* Friendship Press, 1940.

INDEX

26727